THE BIRMINGHAM
COLOURING BOOK

First published 2016

The History Press
The Mill, Brimscombe Port
Stroud, Gloucestershire, GL5 2QG
www.thehistorypress.co.uk

British Library Cataloguing in Publication Data.
A catalogue record for this book is available from the British Library.

ISBN 978 0 7509 7025 9

Cover colouring by Martin Latham.
Typesetting and origination by The History Press
Printed and bound in Great Britain by TJ International Ltd.

THE BIRMINGHAM
COLOURING BOOK

PAST AND PRESENT

Take some time out of your busy life to relax and unwind with this feel-good colouring book designed for everyone who loves Birmingham.

Absorb yourself in the simple action of colouring in the scenes and settings from around the city of Birmingham, past and present. From iconic landmarks and cultural and industrial architecture to picturesque canals and parks, you are sure to find some of your favourite locations waiting to be transformed with a splash of colour.

There are no rules – choose any page and any choice of colouring pens or pencils you like to create your own unique, colourful and creative illustrations.

Selfridges at Bullring Shopping Centre ▸

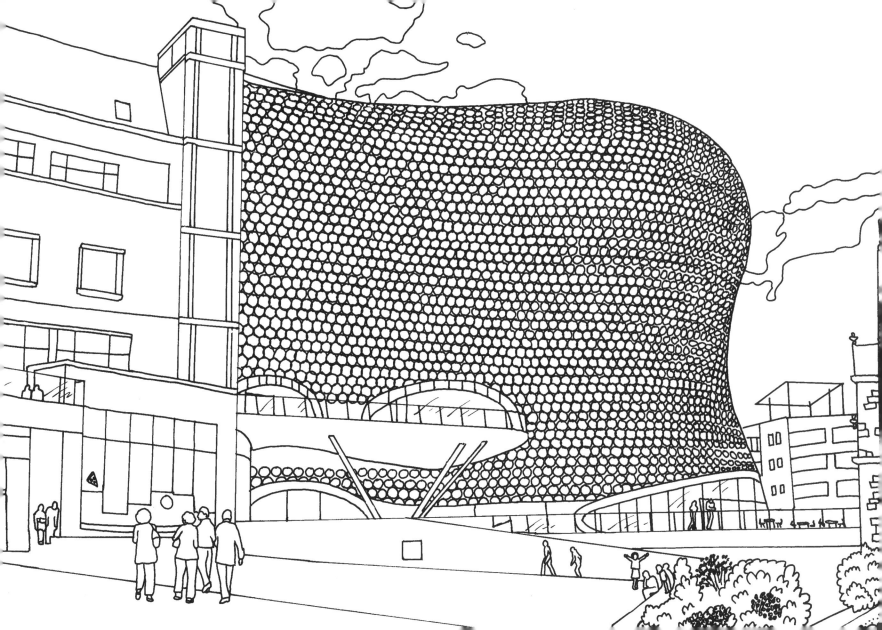

Chancellor's Court, University of Birmingham ▸

Birmingham Botanical Gardens ▸

A tram on the number 40 route at King's Heath Village, 1948 ▸

The Library of Birmingham, Centenary Square ▸

Brindleyplace ▶

The canal wharf at Lifford at the turn of the century ▸

Market stalls at the Bull Ring ▶

Birmingham New Street Station ▶

Birmingham's St Patrick's Day Parade is the largest in Europe outside Dublin ▸

Blakesley Hall, Yardley ▶

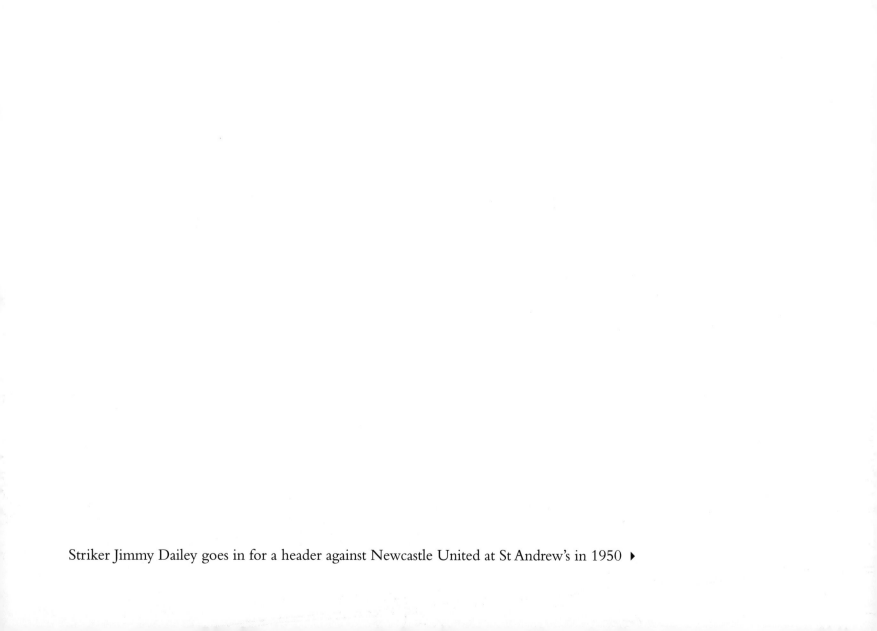

Striker Jimmy Dailey goes in for a header against Newcastle United at St Andrew's in 1950 ▸

Mini Clubmans on the production line at Longbridge in the 1960s ▶

Birmingham Museum and Art Gallery, Chamberlain Square ▸

The Bull Ring Centre in 1970 ▸

Sutton Park ▶

Bull sculpture at Bullring Shopping Centre ▸

Cadbury World, Bournville ▸

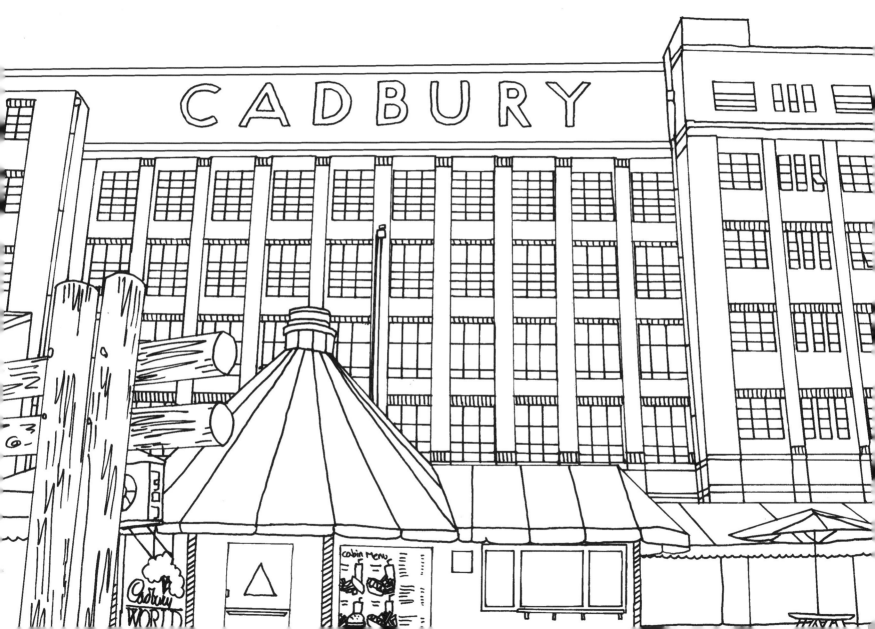

Lily Place, Gem Street, 1930 ▸

Old Turn Junction, where the Birmingham and Fazeley Canal
meets the Birmingham Canal Navigations Main Line Canal ▸

Harborne railway station, 1950 ▸

The Midland Arcade in the Edwardian period ▸

Sarehole Mill, Hall Green ▸

Feeding the geese at Handsworth Park ▶

St Martin in the Bull Ring ▶

The Cube, Wharfside Street ▶

Red panda at Birmingham Wildlife Conservation Park ▸

Museum of the Jewellery Quarter, Vyse Street ▸

Soho House in Handsworth was the home of entrepreneur
Matthew Boulton from 1766 until his death in 1809 ▸

Birmingham Council House ▶

Birmingham Town Hall, Victoria Square ▸

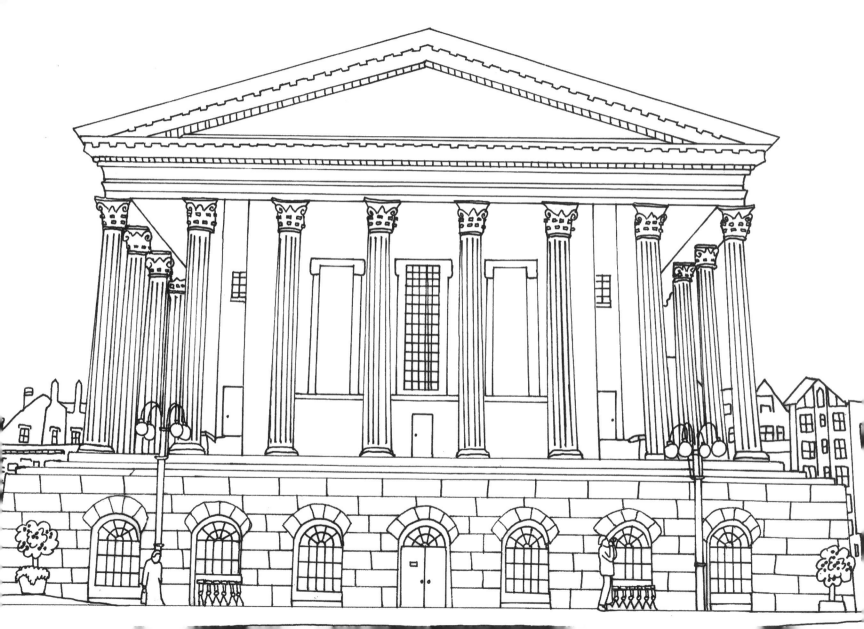

Bull Ring markets ▶

St Philip's Cathedral ▸

Sarlacc Jellyfish at the National Sea Life Centre ▸

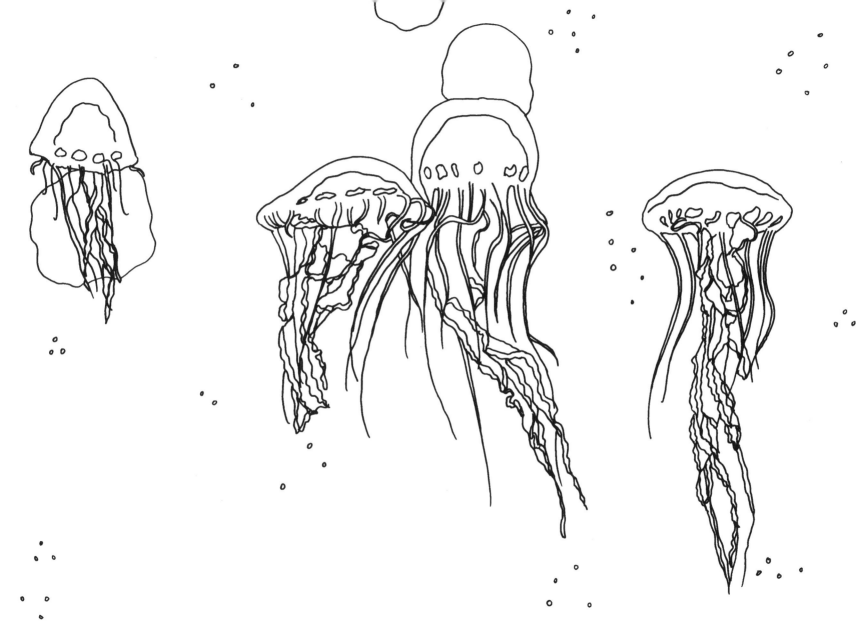

The Old Grammar School at Saint Nicholas' Place, Kings Norton ▸

The bandstand in Handsworth Park, 1920 ▶

Birmingham International Marathon ▸

Villa Cross Picture House, Handsworth, 1962 ▸

Aston Hall, a Grade I listed Jacobean house in Aston ▶

The Hall of Memory, 1937 ▸

Worcester Wharf ▸

The Barber Institute of Fine Arts ▶

Erdington High Street, 1928 ▸

Birmingham & Midland Institute, Margaret Street ▸

Canal cruises outside the International Convention Centre, 1991 ▶